LETO'S HIDDEN TWINS:
ARTEMIS
AND APOLLO

MYTHOLOGY BOOK FOR KIDS

GREEK & ROMAN PAST AND PRESENT SOCIETIES

www.ProfessorBeaver.ca

Published by Speedy Publishing Canada Limited

CONTENTS

In this book, we're going to talk about the story of Leto's hidden twins, Artemis and Apollo, from Greek mythology.

So, let's get right to it!

ARTEMIS - Greek goddess of the hunt, forests and hills, the moon, and archery

APOLLO - Greek god of music, poetry, art, oracles, archery, plague, medicine, sun, light and knowledge

CHAPTER
1

WHO WAS LETO?

Leto was a goddess in Greek mythology. Her parents were a Titan couple. Her father was Coeus, the Titan of the stars and intelligence, and her mother Phoebe, was the goddess of intelligence as well as brightness.

LETO - Titan goddess

ZEUS - god of the sky, ruler of the Olympian gods.

Zeus was the son of two other Titans. His father was Cronus, the god of time and the Titan's leader, and his mother was Rhea, who ruled over fertility and motherhood.

So, Leto was the daughter of a Titan couple

and Zeus was the son of a Titan couple.

Zeus became the leader of the gods on Mount Olympus. The Olympian gods became the rulers of the Greek world after the Titans were dethroned.

Zeus was very powerful and he had romances with many different goddesses as well as mortals. Leto became pregnant with Zeus's

ZEUS - *god of the sky*

children, but despite this, Zeus married Hera.

Even though Zeus had been involved with Leto before Hera was his wife, Hera was very jealous of Leto and set out to cause her some destruction.

This was a pattern with Hera throughout all Greek mythology. Whenever she found out about another one of Zeus's romances she went after the goddess or mortal involved for revenge.

HERA - goddess of marriage

Peacock feathers, the symbol for Hera

CHAPTER
2

HERA SEEKS REVENGE FOR LETO'S PREGNANCY

Zeus saw that Hera was watching his activities so he changed himself and Leto into two quails so they could hide in the

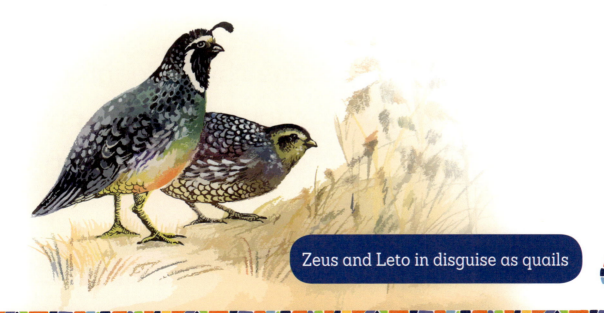

Zeus and Leto in disguise as quails

bushes of the forest.

The quails were brown with speckled feathers

so they were able to blend into the bushes and not be seen, but this didn't fool Hera.

She saw through their change and she put a curse on the beautiful Leto.

HERA - *goddess of marriage*

She told her that she wouldn't be able to give birth anywhere where the sun was shining.

Hera was very powerful, but she couldn't be in all places at all times so she sent the giant monster serpent called Python to help her enforce this horrible curse on Leto. The

Peacock feather, the symbol for Hera

serpent pursued Leto and drove her away as soon as she came out into the sun.

Zeus was concerned about Leto and her unborn child, which was his son or daughter.

He sent a strong south wind to carry her away to an island that was known as Delos. It was a tiny, very rocky island, but the serpent Python continued to pursue Leto.

PYTHON - Giant mythical snake

Silhouette of Artemis hunting

CHAPTER
3

LETO FINALLY GIVES BIRTH

Luckily, the island was so small that the south wind was able to push it more quickly than the serpent could swim, so Leto was finally able to have her baby. She didn't know it but she was carrying twins.

She gave birth to the first twin, a lovely baby daughter. She named

An illustration depicting the Greek goddess Artemis

her daughter Artemis. However, she was so weak and exhausted from all the trials she had gone through that she was having trouble giving birth to the second twin.

Even though Artemis was just a baby, she was already a goddess, so she helped her mother Leto give birth to her twin brother, Apollo.

Greek vase with national ornaments and with the image of Apollo and Artemis.

Ancient Leto sculpture.

Over the years, Zeus had many children but he loved these twins more than the others. They were both beautiful children.

Apollo had hair that was like spun gold and blue eyes the color of the sea. He was a talented musician and poet. He also excelled in medicine and mathematics. He became the sun god as well as a patron of all the arts and sciences.

3D digital render of Artemis the ancient goddess of the hunt

Apollo had strengths and weaknesses just like the other gods, but he was not only handsome, he also had an admirable character. He only told the truth.

Greek mythology states that Apollo was the god who established the famous oracle at Delphi, which is a location in the central part of Greece.

The oracle was a priestess who predicted the future, so Greek citizens from all walks of life, both kings and commoners, came to Delphi to find out the truth. However, the predictions of danger or disaster she gave were sometimes hard to interpret.

The followers of the god Apollo looked into their own hearts and practiced moderation in order to attain wisdom. However, even though Apollo was worshipped and admired, he wasn't perfect. Sometimes he even angered his father Zeus with his jealousy, anger, or cruelty.

Statue of Apollo, son of Zeus

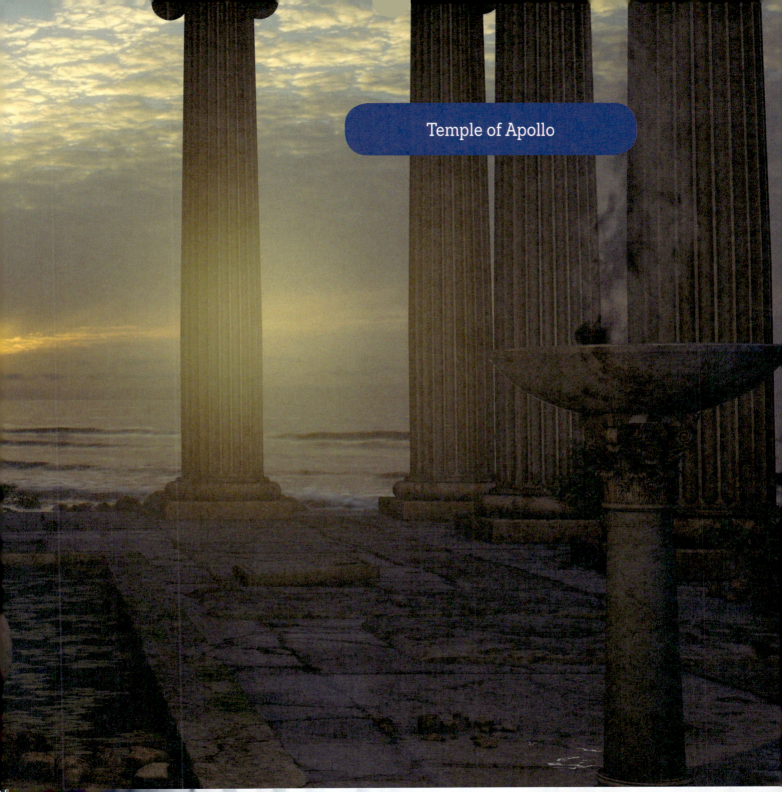

Temple of Apollo

CHAPTER
4

APOLLO GOES IN SEARCH OF PYTHON

Both Apollo and his sister Artemis became masterful at archery. Zeus gave Apollo a golden bow with golden arrows and as soon as Apollo was an expert archer he went in search of Python to

An illustration depicting the Greek god Apollo

kill it.

An illustration depicting the Greek god Apollo

He wanted to seek revenge on the horrible beast that had caused his mother Leto so much pain. Apollo found the Python at the base of Mount Parnassus. He raced up the side of the mountain and shot a fiery arrow, which struck the giant serpent.

The monster screamed in agony and left behind a trail of blood as it slithered into the cave at Delphi, which was considered to be a sacred place belonging to Mother Earth. Apollo couldn't follow the beast inside there, since it was a

An illustration depicting the Greek god Apollo

39

sanctuary where fighting was forbidden.

So, instead he breathed on his fiery arrows to create smoke and filled the cave with the smoky fumes. The beast emerged out of the cave and Apollo killed it and kept its hide as a souvenir of his revenge.

However, Mother Earth was upset that Apollo had killed the beast so close to the sacred cave. She went to Zeus with her complaints so Apollo made amends by naming the annual sports performed

The sun with face of the greek god Apollo.

at Delphi the Pythian Games.

It was a really clever way to announce his own victory over the beast. He also named the priestesses who were oracles at Delphi, the title of Pythonesses.

The ruins of Athina Pronaia temple in Ancient Delphi

Statue of hunting goddess Artemis

CHAPTER
5

THE WISH OF ARTEMIS

Zeus loved his son, Apollo, but he also loved his daughter Artemis. Apollo seemed to be bathed in a golden light, but Artemis had a beautiful silvery sheen to her. When she was three years old, Zeus asked her

An illustration depicting the Greek goddess Artemis

An illustration depicting the Greek goddess Artemis

what she wanted and she made an unusual set of wishes.

She had decided that she always wanted to be a young girl and never be given in marriage to any mortal or god. She also wanted a silver bow with silver arrows and the freedom to hunt wild and free in the mountains with a pack of fierce hunting hounds. Zeus told her that she could have her wishes.

Artemis went to the god of the forge to get her silver bow and arrows. His name was Hephaestus. [Hu-fay-stus] But he couldn't make them for her. He

The smith god Hephaestus

said that such a bow with its accompanying arrows would need to be forged under the water bathed in cold light.

A cyclops tending a flock of sheep

So, Artemis went to the sea to ask the Cyclopes, who were one-eyed creatures, responsible for creating Zeus's thunderbolts. They fashioned the beautiful, magical

sigh-clo-peas

arrows, quiver, and bows for her. As soon as the quiver that held the arrows was empty, it filled up with arrows again.

Then, she went to Pan, the god of the mountains

Artemis with her hunting hounds

and shepherds. He offered her his ten best bloodhounds. From then forward, Artemis spent her days running through the forest hunting deer and racing across the sky. She was worshipped as the maiden goddess of the moon and the stars. The men who decided to pursue her were chased away by her pack of lively bloodhounds. She lived alone but was content with her life.

In Roman mythology, she is known as Diana and many artists painted and sculpted her as she carried her silver bow and arrows. She was often shown with her loyal dogs around her.

Sometimes when young women didn't want to be married off to someone they didn't love, they prayed to the goddess Artemis to save them. According to many Greek legends, Artemis saved these women, but she turned them into parts of the forest, such as trees or deer.

Evidently, the Greeks believed that it was better to become a magical plant or animal than to be married to a spouse one didn't love.

Ancient sculpture of the goddess-hunter Artemis

Signboard of The Altar of Apollo, it is built of Parian marble, Delphi, Greece.

CHAPTER
6

SUMMARY

Zeus, the god of all the Olympian gods, had a romance with Leto who was a Titan goddess. She became pregnant with Zeus's child, but Zeus went forward to marry the goddess Hera. When Hera found out about Leto, she went into a fury and sent the beast Python to make it impossible for Leto to give birth.

Eventually, Zeus sent the south wind to help Leto and she ended up on a rocky island where she gave birth to her daughter

Artemis and eventually to Apollo, Artemis's twin brother.

Both Apollo and Artemis were very beautiful and talented in many different fields, especially archery. In Roman mythology, Artemis was known as Diana.

Awesome! Now that you've read about the story of Artemis and Apollo, you may want to read another mythology story in the Baby Professor book Cronus Swallowed His Children! Mythology 4th Grade | Children's

Greek & Roman Book.

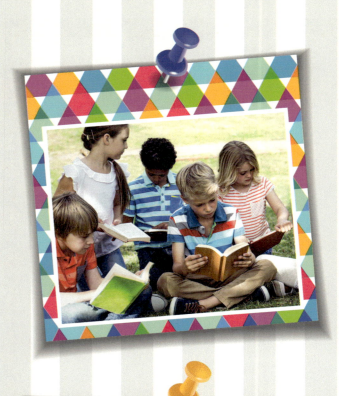

Made in United States
Cleveland, OH
14 February 2025